# Sharks

by Martha E. H. Rustad

Consulting Editor: Gail Saunders-Smith, Ph.D.

Consultant: Jody Byrum, Science Writer,
SeaWorld Education Department

## Pebble Books

an imprint of Capstone Press
Mankato, Minnesota

Pebble Books are published by Capstone Press
151 Good Counsel Drive, P.O. Box 669, Mankato, Minnesota 56002
http://www.capstone-press.com

1 2 3 4 5 6 06 05 04 03 02 01

*Library of Congress Cataloging-in-Publication Data*
Rustad, Martha E. H. (Martha Elizabeth Hillman), 1975–
    Sharks / by Martha E. H. Rustad.
    p. cm.—(Ocean life)
    Includes bibliographical references (p. 23) and index.
    ISBN 0-7368-0861-2
    1. Sharks—Juvenile literature. [1. Sharks.] I. Title. II. Series.
QL638.9 .R87 2001
597.3—dc21

                                                                00-009864

Summary: Simple text and photographs present sharks and their behavior.

## Note to Parents and Teachers

The Ocean Life series supports national science standards for units on the diversity and unity of life. The series shows that animals have features that help them live in different environments. This book describes sharks and illustrates how they live. The photographs support early readers in understanding the text. The repetition of words and phrases helps early readers learn new words. This book also introduces early readers to subject-specific vocabulary words, which are defined in the Words to Know section. Early readers may need assistance to read some words and to use the Table of Contents, Words to Know, Read More, Internet Sites, and Index/Word List sections of the book.

# Table of Contents

Sharks are fish.

Sharks breathe
through gills.

Sharks have rough skin.

fins

fins

Sharks have fins.

Sharks move their tail
back and forth to swim.

Sharks hunt prey.

Some sharks have strong jaws.

Some sharks have
rows of sharp teeth.

Sharks eat ocean animals.

# Words to Know

**fin**—a body part without bones that fish use to swim; sharks have pectoral, pelvic, dorsal, anal, and caudal fins.

**fish**—a cold-blooded animal that lives in water and has scales, fins, and gills; unlike most fish, sharks have skeletons made of cartilage instead of bone.

**gill**—a body part that fish use to breathe

**hunt**—to find and kill animals for food; sharks hunt by hearing, smelling, and feeling prey.

**jaw**—a body part that holds teeth; the upper jaw of a shark can separate from the skull; sharks then can swallow large prey.

**prey**—an animal that is hunted and eaten; sharks eat fish as well as plankton, seals, and other sharks.

**rough**—not smooth; dermal denticles are the small, rough scales that cover sharks' skin.

**teeth**—the hard, white mouthparts used to bite food; sharks do not chew their food.

# Read More

**Bauman, Amy, and Patricia Corrigan.** *The Wonder of Sharks.* Animal Wonders. Milwaukee: Gareth Stevens, 2000.

**Fine, John Christopher.** *Diving with Sharks.* New York: Franklin Watts, 2000.

**Schaefer, Lola M.** *Sharks: Hunters of the Deep.* The Wild World of Animals. Mankato, Minn.: Bridgestone Books, 2001.

# Internet Sites

**The Search for Ancient Sharks**
http://www.discovery.com/exp/prehistoricsharks/prehistoricsharks.html

**Sharks and Their Relatives**
http://www.seaworld.org/Sharks/pageone.html

**What Is a Shark?**
http://www.EnchantedLearning.com/subjects/sharks

# Index/Word List

**Word Count: 42**
**Early-Intervention Level: 6**

**Credits**
Steve Christensen, cover designer and illustrator; Kia Bielke, production designer;
   Kimberly Danger, photo researcher

Dale Knuepfer/Bruce Coleman Inc., 12
Dave Fleetham/Tom Stack & Associates, 6, 18
Ed Robinson/Tom Stack & Associates, 10
Norbert Wu/www.norbertwu.com, 8
Norman Owen Tomalin/Bruce Coleman Inc., 4
Photo Network/Hal Beral, 20
Randy Morse/Tom Stack & Associates, 1, 14
Visuals Unlimited/David Fleetham, cover, 16